CVN-75 Harry S. Truman, U.S. Navy Aircraft Carrier

By W. Frederick Zimmerman

NIMBLE BOOKS LLC

NIMBLE BOOKS LLC

ISBN-13: 978-1-934840-26-9

ISBN-10: 1-934840-26-2

Copyright 2008 W. Frederick Zimmerman

Version 1.0; last saved 2008-08-26.

Nimble Books LLC

1521 Martha Avenue

Ann Arbor, MI 48103-5333

http://www.nimblebooks.com

Photographs by U.S. Navy personnel in the performance of their official duties except for photographs of the LEGO version of CVN-75, which are © and courtesy Malle Hawking.

Contents

Nimble Books LLC

Introduction

This "nimble" book gives you a unique keepsake with 32 beautifully color printed images of U.S.S. *Harry S. Truman,* CVN-75.

Buy This Book If:

- You want a permanent, printed collection of beautiful, thought-provoking images of *Truman.*
- You want the perfect gift for a friend, family member, or shipmate.
- You love Harry Truman, Presidents, the U.S. Navy, naval aviation, or aircraft carriers.

SPECIFICATIONS

Displacement: 101,000 to 104,000 tons full load

Length: Overall: 1,092 ft (333 m), waterline: 1,040 ft (317 m)

Beam: Overall: 252 ft (76.8 m), waterline: 134 ft (40.8 m)

Draft: Maximum navigational: 37 ft (11.3 m); limit: 41 ft (12.5 m)

Propulsion: 2 × Westinghouse A4W nuclear reactors, 4 × steam turbines, 4 × shafts, 260,000 shp (194 MW)

Speed: 30+ knots (56+ km/h)

Range: Essentially unlimited

Complement: Ship's company: 3,200

Air wing: 2,480

Armament: 2 × Mk 29 Sea Sparrow, 2 × RIM-116 Rolling Airframe Missile

Aircraft carried: 90 fixed wing and helicopters

Motto: *The Buck Stops Here*

Nickname: *HST*

IMAGES

Figure 1. The ship's seal.

Figure 2. The ship's battle flag, modeled after the battle flag of the 129th Field Artillery Regiment, 35th Infantry Division, in which Captain Harry S. Truman was a battery commander during World War I.

Figure 3. Sea trials, 1998.

Figure 4. Cross-section, 1999.

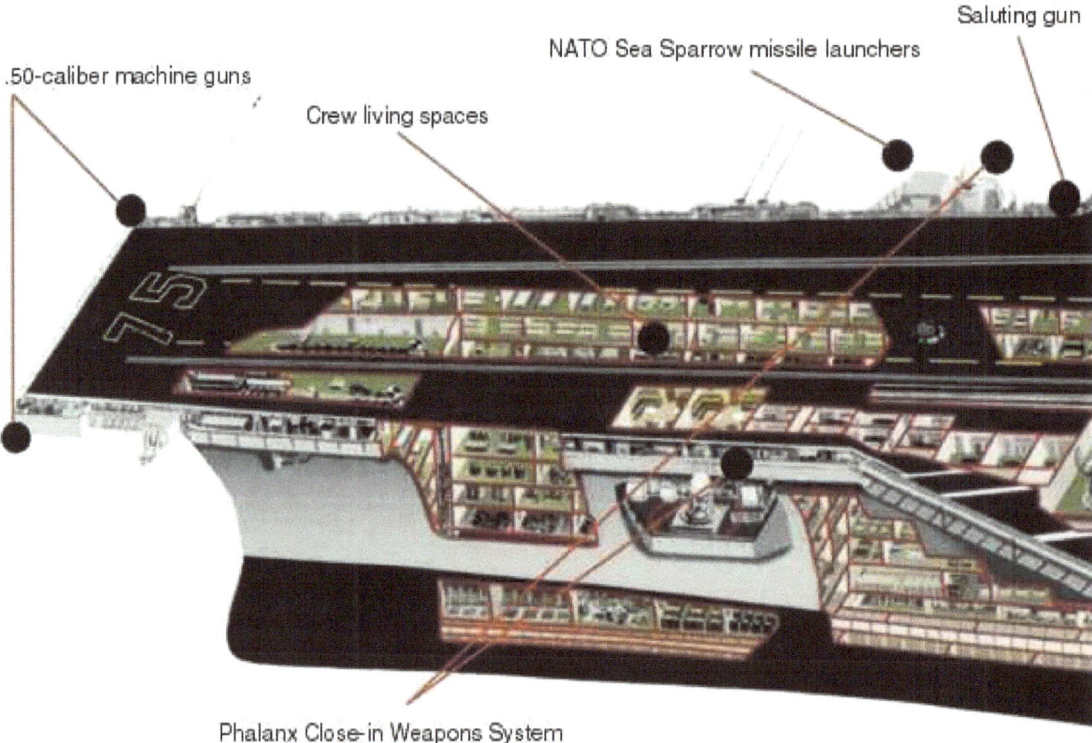

.50-caliber machine guns

Crew living spaces

NATO Sea Sparrow missile launchers

Saluting gun

Phalanx Close-in Weapons System

Figure 5. Cross-section (bow).

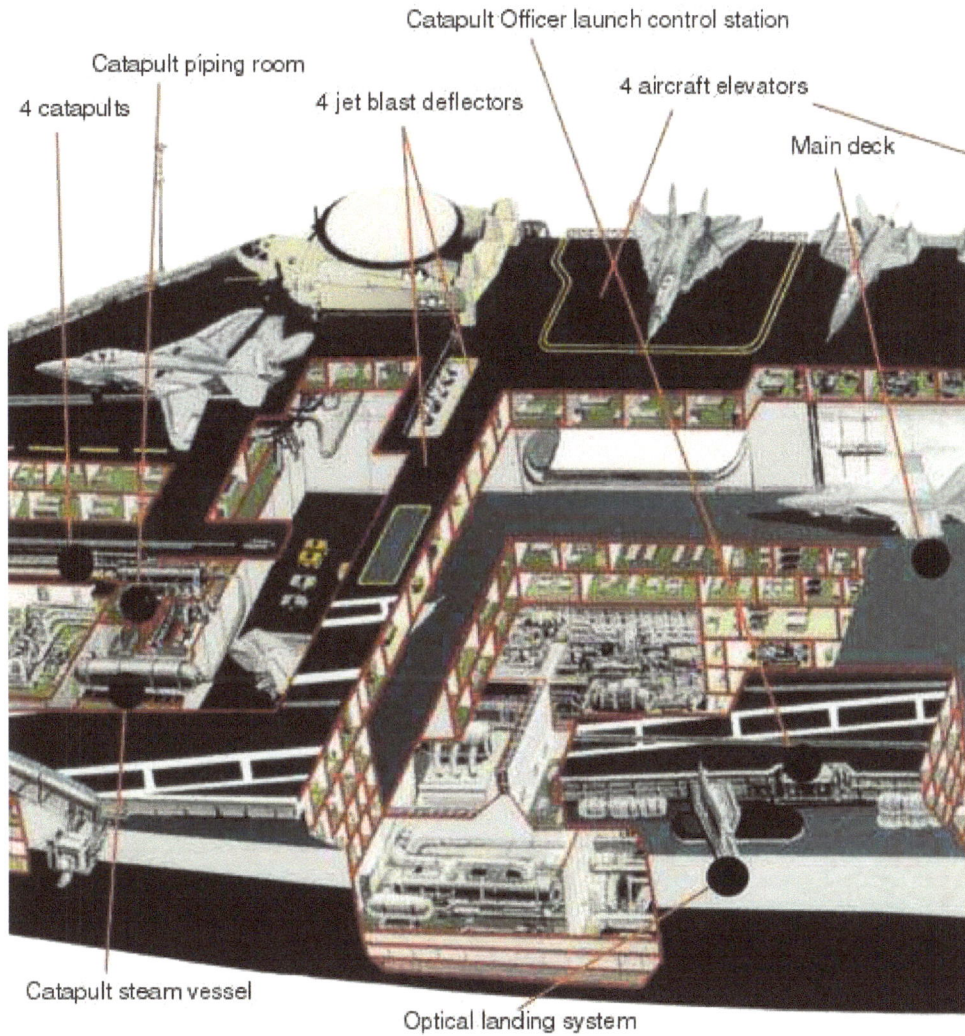

Figure 6. Cross-section, moving aft.

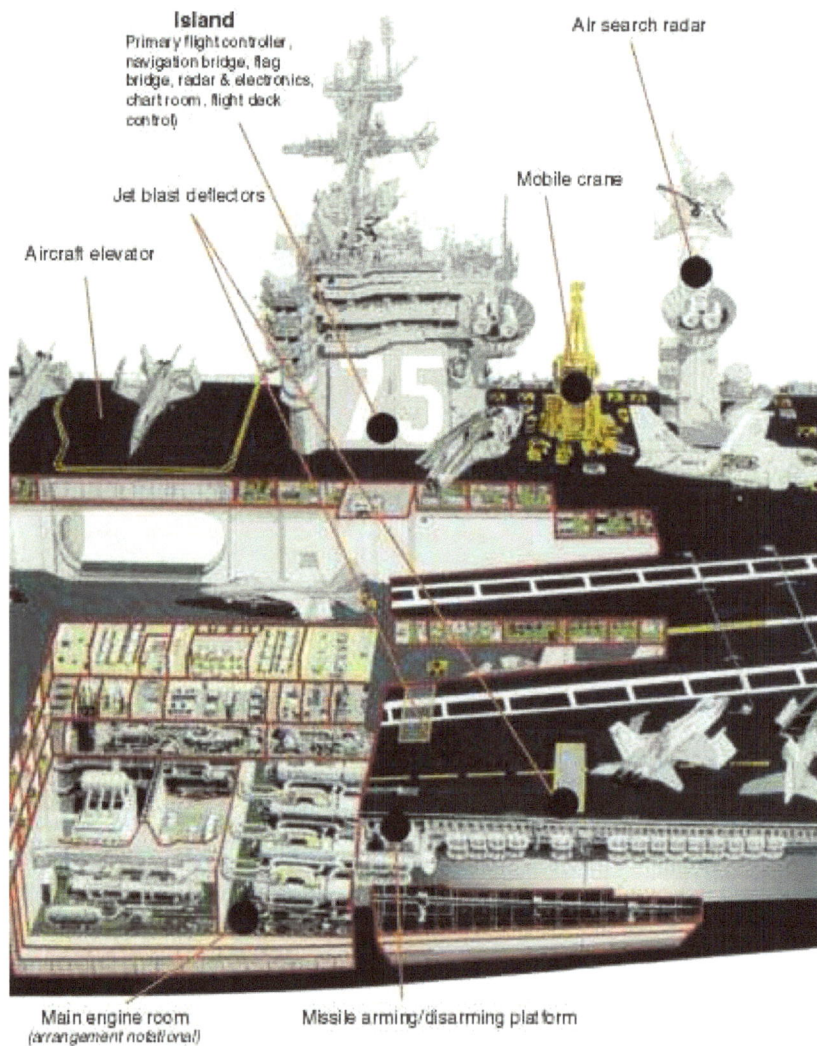

Island
Primary flight controller,
navigation bridge, flag
bridge, radar & electronics,
chart room, flight deck
control)

Air search radar

Jet blast deflectors

Mobile crane

Aircraft elevator

Main engine room
(arrangement notational)

Missile arming/disarming platform

Figure 7. Cross-section at the island.

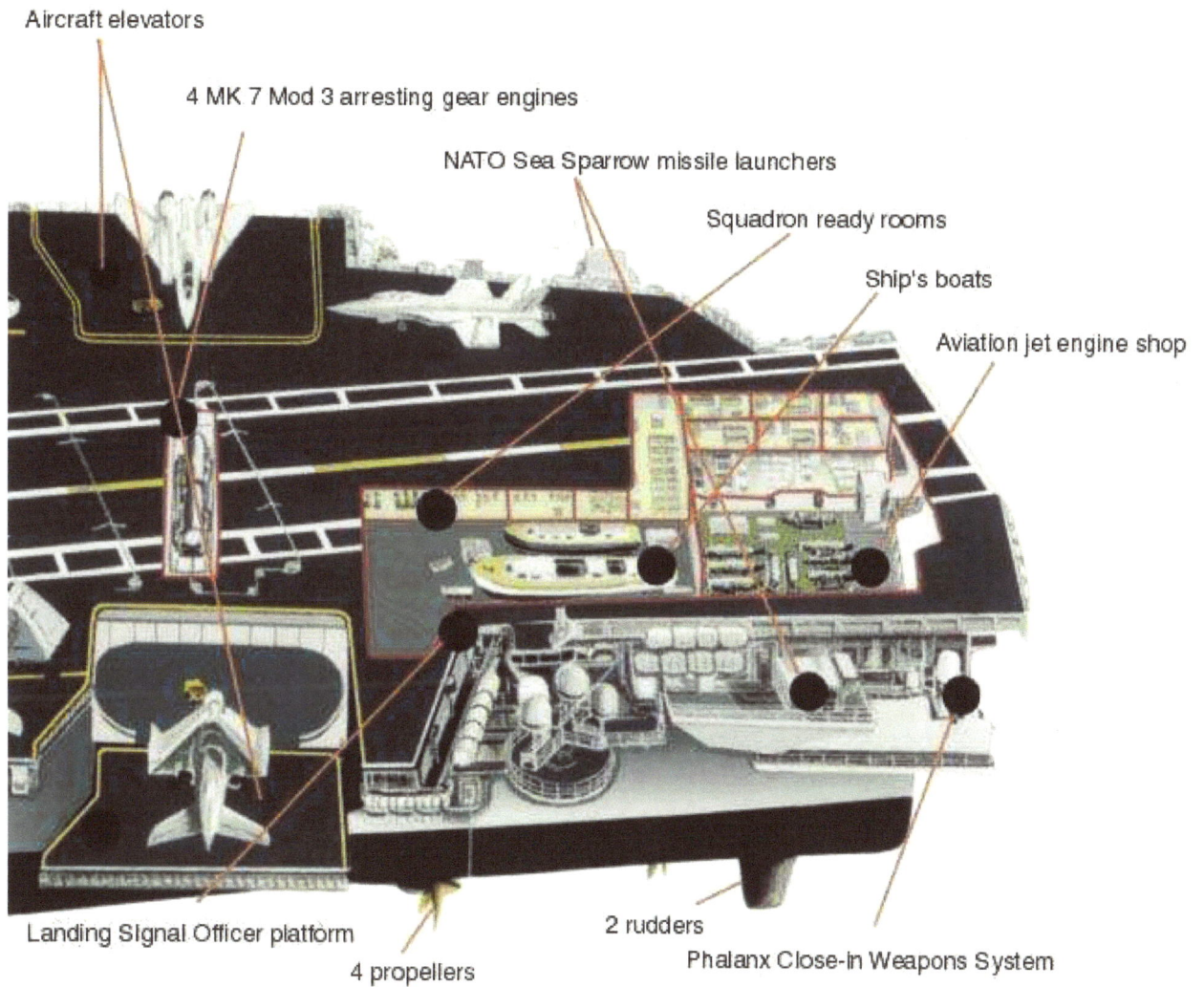

Aircraft elevators

4 MK 7 Mod 3 arresting gear engines

NATO Sea Sparrow missile launchers

Squadron ready rooms

Ship's boats

Aviation jet engine shop

Landing Signal Officer platform

4 propellers

2 rudders

Phalanx Close-in Weapons System

Figure 8. Cross-section at the stern.

Figure 9. A 21-gun salute at Truman's commissioning, July 25, 1998.

Figure 10. A glimpse of scale relative to Halifax, Nova Scotia. 1999.

Figure 11. This aerial view gives a different perspective on scale. 2002.

Figure 12. Another port visit, Suda Bay, Crete, 2002.

Figure 13. Leaving Suda Bay, 2004.

Figure 14. Old-style Portsmouth, England, 2005.

Figure 15. Manning the rails to honor the sailors who fought in the Battle of Midway on its 60th anniversary, June 4, 2002.

Figure 16. Times change. Harry S. Truman's predecessor oversaw the conquest of Axis Italy. Now *Truman* is operating together with the Italian carrier *Giuseppe Garibaldi*, 2004.

Figure 17. A bit crowded in here! F/A-18 Hornets in the hangar during a no-fly day, 2005.

Figure 18. The "Ouija Board" is a model of the flight deck used to help position aircraft during operations. 2005.

Figure 19. Fire fighting training amid emergency lights and simulated smoke, 2004.

Figure 20. Firefighting aboard ship is brutal and frightening stuff. 2007.

Figure 21. Conducting flight operations, 2008.

Figure 22. Launching an aircraft, 2006.

Figure 23. Night operations, February 2001.

Figure 24. The pointy end of the big stick. GBU-12 laser-guided bombs being loaded on board an F-14 Tomcat, 2005.

Figure 25. A screech owl found living on board, in an aircraft wheel well. 2008.

Figure 26. The obligatory dusk shot. 2002.

Figure 27. And now for something completely different: a LEGO model of Truman with its creator, Malle Hawking. (Photo courtesy Hawking).

Figure 28. Some of the amazing interior detail.
(photo courtesy Malle Hawking)

Figure 29. Comin' at ya! (photo courtesy Malle Hawking).

NAMESAKE

Figure 30. President Harry S. Truman.

IT'S HARRY "S." TRUMAN

According to the Harry S. Truman Presidential Library:

In recent years the question of whether to use a period after the "S" in Harry S. Truman's name has become a subject of controversy, especially among editors. The evidence provided by Mr. Truman's own practice argues strongly for the use of the period. While, as many people do, Mr. Truman often ran the letters in his signature together in a single stroke, the archives of the Harry S. Truman Library have numerous examples of the signature written at various times throughout Mr. Truman's lifetime where his use of a period after the "S" is very obvious.

Mr. Truman apparently initiated the "period" controversy in 1962 when, perhaps in jest, he told newspapermen that the period should be omitted. In explanation he said that the "S" did not stand for any name but was a compromise between the names of his grandfathers, Anderson Shipp Truman and Solomon Young. He was later heard to say that the use of the period dated after 1962 as well as before.

Several widely recognized style manuals provide guidance in favor of using the period. According to The Chicago Manual of Style all initials given with a name should "for convenience and consistency" be followed by a period even if they are not abbreviations of names. The U.S. Government Printing Office Style Manual states that the period should be used after the "S" in Harry S. Truman's name.

Most published works using the name Harry S. Truman employ the period. Authors choosing to omit the period in their texts must still use it when citing the names of organizations that employ the period in their legal titles (e.g. Harry S. Truman Library) thus seeming to contradict themselves. Authoritative publications produced by the Government Printing Office consistently use the period in Mr. Truman's name, notably the Department of State's documentary series Foreign Relations of the United States, Diplomatic Papers, the Department of the Army's United States Army in World War II and two major publications of the

Office of the Federal Register, Public Papers of the President - Harry S. Truman and the United States Government Organization Manual. [1]

Figure 31. Harry S. Truman's signature, with the "."

Figure 32. Note the period after the "S" painted on the ship.

---

[1] http://www.trumanlibrary.org/speriod.htm

NIMBLE BOOKS LLC

A LETTER FROM THE PUBLISHER

Dear Reader,

I am pleased to bring you this latest volume in the Modern Warships series from Nimble Books, which marks an important milestone in that it completes our set of pictorial books about *Nimitz* class carriers. I especially like the LEGO pictures from Malle Hawking!

Next up: a few more modern warships, including a definitive book about the English CV-Fs (Aircraft Carrier, Future) *Prince of Wales* and *Queen Elizabeth II* from Tim Mahon, a defence correspondent in the U.K.; *DDG-1000 R.I.P.*; and *The Arsenal Ship*, moving with the last two into the entertaining territory of hypothetical and "never were" ships.

If you like the Modern Warships books, you may also enjoy our books about World War Two ships, including *Battleship Yamato: Why She Matters Today; BB-67 Montana;* and Wayne Scarpaci's illustrated history of proposed *Iowa-* and *Alaska*-class conversions. Visit www.NimbleBooks.com for our latest list!

-Fred Zimmerman, Nimble Books LLC
Ann Arbor, Michigan, USA, August 26, 2008